chicken buffet

Which came first—the chicken, or the recipe?

If you ask the design team of Linda Huber and Bonnie Collins, the answer is likely to be: **"The quilt came first!"**

Linda and Bonnie have been friends for almost a decade now. The designing duo met while working on quilts for Project Linus, the popular charity that provides blankets for children.

"I've been quilting and teaching since 1993," says Linda. "Before that, I started sewing garments when I was five years old. Bonnie is excellent at decorative needlework and has done that for many years, so the Chicken Buffet quilt was the perfect team project for the two of us."

As for the question of which came first, the design work actually started with the chicken. The food theme evolved out of the humorous designs.

"At the last minute," Linda explains, "we decided to include recipes with the patterns. Bonnie worked hard to gather the recipes that go with each block."

So what's next for Linda & Bonnie?

Linda chuckled before answering. "We've gone back to working on our personal projects while we wait to see how this book is received."

And although it usually is wise to refrain from counting chickens or book sales ahead of time, we're betting that this upbeat mix of frolicking fowls and delicious dishes will fly off the shelves and into the hands of quilters and cooks everywhere.

For a wide variety of quilt and appliqué ideas that will help you feather your nest quite nicely, visit www.leisurearts.com.

LEISURE ARTS, INC.
Little Rock, Arkansas

chicken buffet quilt

Finished Quilt Size: 52" x 66½" (132 cm x 169 cm)
Finished Block Size: 12" x 12" (30 cm x 30 cm)

FABRIC REQUIREMENTS

Yardage is based on 43"/44" (109 cm/112 cm) wide fabric.

- ³/₄ yd (69 cm) of dark purple batik for outer border
- ³/₄ yd (69 cm) of medium purple batik for sashing squares and binding
- ³/₄ yd (69 cm) of light purple batik for block backgrounds
- 1¹/₈ yds (1 m) of light purple striped batik for sashing strips
- ³/₄ yd (69 cm) of light purple floral batik for block backgrounds and star centers
- ¹/₈ yd (11 cm) **each** of 3 purple tone-on-tone prints for star points
- 1³/₈ yds (1.3 m) of blue batik for block backgrounds and block labels
- ⁵/₈ yd (57 cm) of black solid for accent strips
- ¹/₄ yd (23 cm) of black print for chicken wings and combs
- ¹/₂ yd (46 cm) of yellow print for chicken bodies
- ¹/₄ yd (23 cm) of orange print for chicken legs
- Assorted fabric scraps for remaining appliqués
- 4¹/₄ yds (3.9 m) of fabric for backing

You will also need:
- 60" x 74½" (152 cm x 189 cm) rectangle of batting
- Paper-backed fusible web
- Stabilizer
- Assorted embellishments - We used seed beads, pearls, sequins, buttons, and rickrack.
- Assorted colors of embroidery floss
- Black fine-point permanent fabric marking pen

CUTTING THE BACKGROUNDS AND BORDERS

Follow **Rotary Cutting**, page 33, to cut fabric. Cut all strips from the selvage-to-selvage width of the fabric. All measurements include ¹/₄" seam allowances.

From dark purple batik:
- Cut 7 **border strips** 3" wide.

From medium purple batik:
- Cut 2 strips 3" wide. From these strips, cut 17 **sashing squares** 3" x 3".
- Cut 7 **binding strips** 2½" wide.

From light purple batik:
- Cut 3 strips 7" wide. From these strips, cut 12 **background squares** 7" x 7".

From light purple striped batik:
- Cut 11 strips 3" wide. From these strips, cut 31 **sashing strips** 3" x 12½".

From light purple floral batik:
- Cut 3 strips 7" wide. From these strips, cut 12 **background squares** 7" x 7" and 3 **sashing squares** 3" x 3".

From each purple tone-on-tone print:
- Cut 1 strip 2" wide. From this strip, cut 8 **rectangles** 2" x 3½".

From blue batik:
- Cut 5 strips 7" wide. From these strips, cut 24 **background squares** 7" x 7".

From black solid:
- Cut 16 strips 1¼" wide. From these strips, cut 48 **accent strips** 1¼ x 12½".

CUTTING THE APPLIQUÉS

Patterns, pages 9 – 31, are reversed and do not include seam allowances. Follow **Preparing Fusible Appliqués**, page 34, to cut appliqués.

From blue batik:
- Cut 12 **block labels** 3" x 7".

From black print, yellow print, orange print, and assorted fabric scraps:
- For each block, cut 1 of each pattern.

MAKING THE BLOCKS

Follow **Piecing** and **Pressing**, page 34, to make the block backgrounds. Use 1/4" seam allowances throughout. Refer to **Block Photos**, pages 8 – 30, for appliqué and embellishment placement. Follow **Machine Blanket Stitch Appliqué**, page 34, for technique. Refer to **Hand Stitches**, page 40, for embroidery techniques.

1. Sew 1 light purple floral batik **square**, 1 light purple batik **square**, and 2 blue batik **squares** together to make **background square**. Make 12 background squares.

Background Square (make 12)

2. Working from background to forefront, arrange appliqués for each Block on a background square; fuse in place.
3. Machine Blanket Stitch Appliqués to background squares to make 12 **Blocks**.

Block (make 12)

4. Keeping appliqués centered, trim each Block to 12 1/2" x 12 1/2".
5. Add desired embellishments and embroidery to each Block.
6. **Note:** Our block labels were machine embroidered using an approximately 3/8" tall font. Other options include writing names on block labels with black marking pen or hand embroidering using black floss.
7. Trim block label 1/4" larger than name on top and left side edges and 3/4" larger than name on bottom and right side edges.
8. Matching bottom and side raw edges, fuse 1 block label to lower left corner of each Block. Machine Blanket Stitch Appliqué block label to Block.

ADDING THE ACCENT STRIPS

Note: The accent strips are not borders between the blocks and sashings; rather the raw edges are stitched into the seam and the folded edge is free (see photo).

1. Matching wrong sides and raw edges, press **accent strips** in half lengthwise.
2. Matching right sides and raw edges, baste 1 accent strip to sides of each Block.
3. Overlapping at corners, baste 1 accent strip to top and bottom edges of each Block.

MAKING THE SILLY STAR SASHING STRIPS

Note: To make each Silly Star Sashing Strip you will use 2 matching rectangles and 1 sashing strip. Angling the placement of the rectangles when sewing them to the sashing strips makes the uneven star points. And to make it even easier don't concern yourself with stitching a consistent 1/4" seam allowance. Just sew a straight line along 1 side of the rectangle.

1. Matching right sides, angle 1 **rectangle** on left corner of 1 **sashing strip** (**Fig. 1**). Sew along outer long edge of rectangle. Open rectangle and press; trim rectangle even with edges of sashing strip (**Fig. 2**). Repeat for right corner (**Fig. 3**).

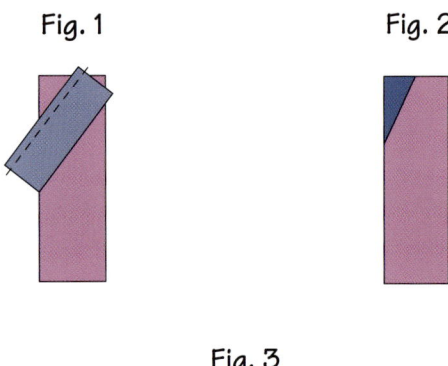

2. Repeat Step 1 to make 12 Silly Star Sashings.

ASSEMBLING THE QUILT TOP CENTER

Follow **Piecing** and **Pressing**, page 34, to assemble quilt top. Use 1/4" seam allowances throughout.

1. Noting placement of Silly Stars, sew 3 **blocks** and 4 **sashing strips** together to make a **Row**. Make 4 Rows.
2. Noting placement of Silly Stars, sew 4 **sashing squares** and 3 **sashing strips** together to make a **Sashing Row**. Make 5 Sashing Rows.
3. Sew Rows and Sashing Rows together to make quilt top center.

ADDING THE BORDERS

1. Using diagonal seams (**Fig. 4**), sew **border strips** together end to end to make 1 continuous border strip.

Fig. 4

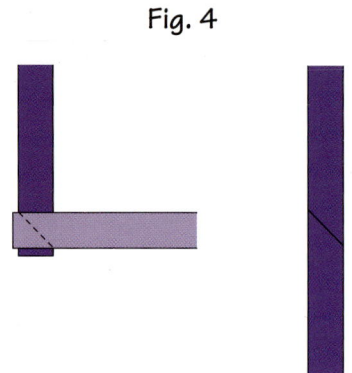

2. To determine length of side borders, measure **length** of quilt top. From border strip, cut 2 **side borders** the determined length. Matching centers and corners, sew side borders to quilt top. Press seam allowances toward borders.
3. To determine length of top/bottom borders, measure **width** of quilt top (including added borders). From border strip, cut 2 **top/bottom borders** the determined length. Matching centers and corners, sew top and bottom borders to quilt top. Press seam allowances toward borders.

FINISHING THE QUILT

1. Following **Quilting**, page 36, to mark, layer, and quilt. Our quilt is quilted with a leaf and vine pattern in the borders and sashings. The stars in the sashings are quilted in the ditch. There is outline quilting around the appliqués. The block backgrounds have a combination of outlining around the flowers of the batik floral and meandering in the remaining areas.
2. Refer to **Making a Hanging Sleeve**, page 38, to make and attach a hanging sleeve, if desired.
3. Use **binding strips** and follow **Binding**, page 38, to bind quilt.

wall hanging

Finished Wall Hanging Size: 19" x 19" (48 cm x 48 cm)
Finished Block Size: 12" x 12" (30 cm x 30 cm)

FABRIC REQUIREMENTS
Yardage is based on 43"/44" (109 cm/112 cm) wide fabric.

Completed block of your choice
¼ yd (23 cm) of fabric for outer border
⅛ yd (11 cm) of fabric for accent strips
22" x 22" (56 cm x 56 cm) backing square
¼ yd (23 cm) of fabric for binding

You will also need:
22" x 22" (56 cm x 56 cm) square of batting

CUTTING THE BACKGROUNDS AND BORDERS
Follow **Rotary Cutting**, page 33, to cut fabric. Cut all strips from the selvage-to-selvage width of the fabric. All measurements include ¼" seam allowances.

From fabric for outer border:
- Cut 2 **side borders** 3½" x 12½".
- Cut 2 **top/bottom borders** 3½" x 18½".

From fabric for accent strips:
- Cut 2 strips 1¼" wide. From these strips, cut 4 **accent strips** 1¼" x 12½".

From fabric for binding:
- Cut 3 **binding strips** 2½" wide.

ADDING THE ACCENT STRIPS
Note: The accent strips are not borders between the blocks and sashings; rather the raw edges are stitched into the seam and the folded edge is free (see photo).

1. Matching wrong sides and raw edges, press **accent strips** in half lengthwise.
2. Matching right sides and raw edges, baste 1 accent strip to sides of each Block.
3. Overlapping at corners, baste 1 accent strip to top and bottom edges of each Block.

ADDING THE BORDERS
1. Matching centers and corners, sew **side borders** to Block. Press seam allowances toward borders.
2. Matching centers and corners, sew **top** and **bottom borders** to Block. Press seam allowances toward borders.

FINISHING THE QUILT
1. Following **Quilting**, page 36, to mark, layer, and quilt. Our wall hanging is quilted in the ditch around each appliqué and with meandering quilting in the block background.
2. Refer to **Making a Hanging Sleeve**, page 38, to make and attach a hanging sleeve, if desired.
3. Use **binding strips** and follow **Binding**, page 38, to bind wall hanging.

Chicken Gumbo

chicken gumbo

3 c. chicken broth
1 c. cubed cooked chicken
1 c. diced tomatoes
8-oz. can tomato sauce
1/3 c. uncooked white rice
1/4 of a green pepper, chopped
1/4 of an onion, chopped
1/2 c. corn
2 tsp. dried basil leaves
1/2 tsp. black pepper
1/2 tsp. garlic salt

Place all ingredients in a soup/stock pot. Bring to a boil. Reduce the heat to a simmer and cook until rice is soft.

Makes 1-2 servings.

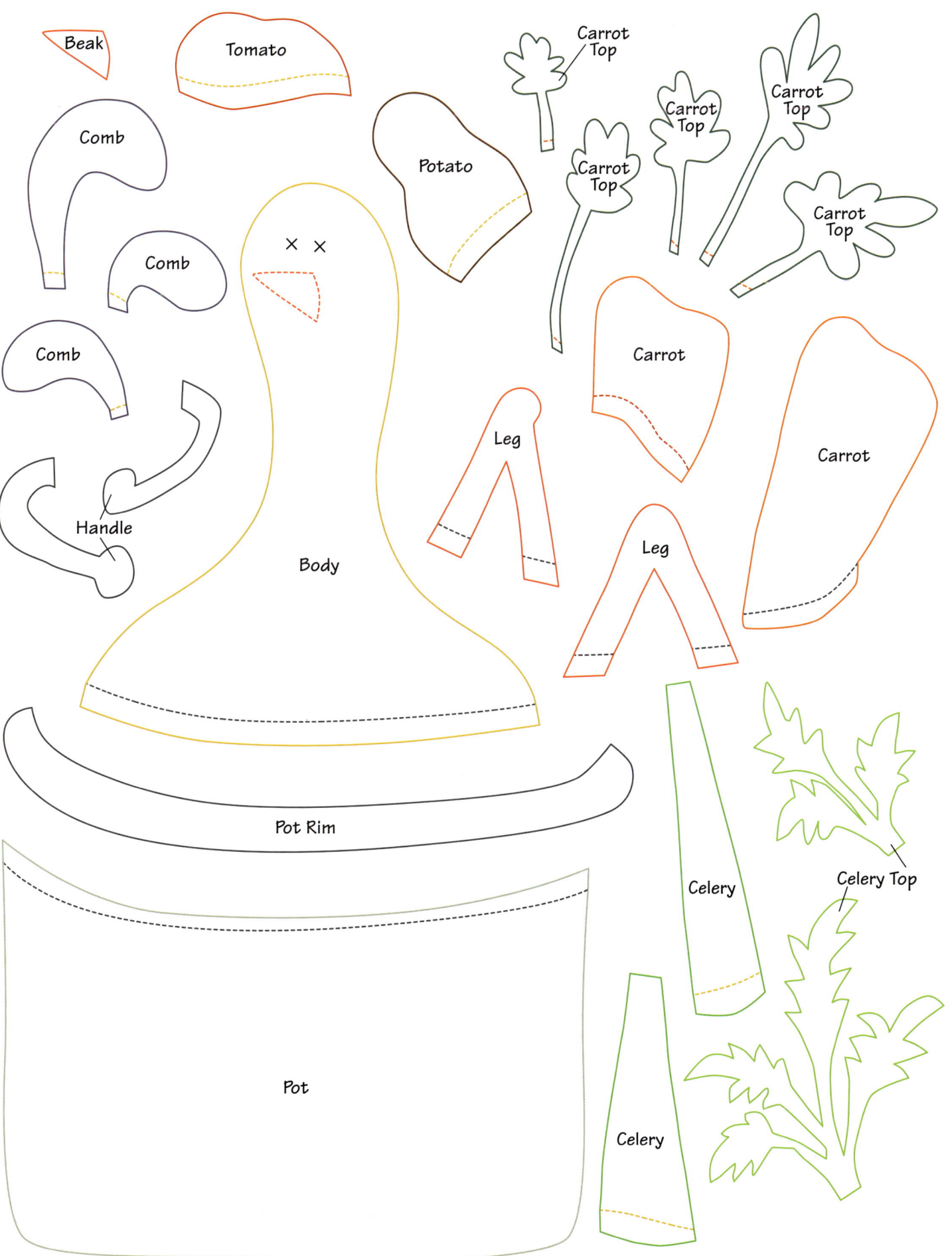

Chicken Divan

chicken divan

2 c. fresh or frozen broccoli
10¾-oz. can cream of mushroom soup
⅓ c. milk
8-oz. shredded cooked chicken breasts
½ c. shredded cheddar cheese

Steam broccoli; drain. Arrange in a shallow baking dish. Over low heat, combine soup and milk in a saucepan; stir until smooth. Layer chicken over broccoli. Pour soup mixture over chicken. Sprinkle cheese on top. Bake in a 450° oven for 25-30 minutes until hot and bubbly.

Makes 2 servings.

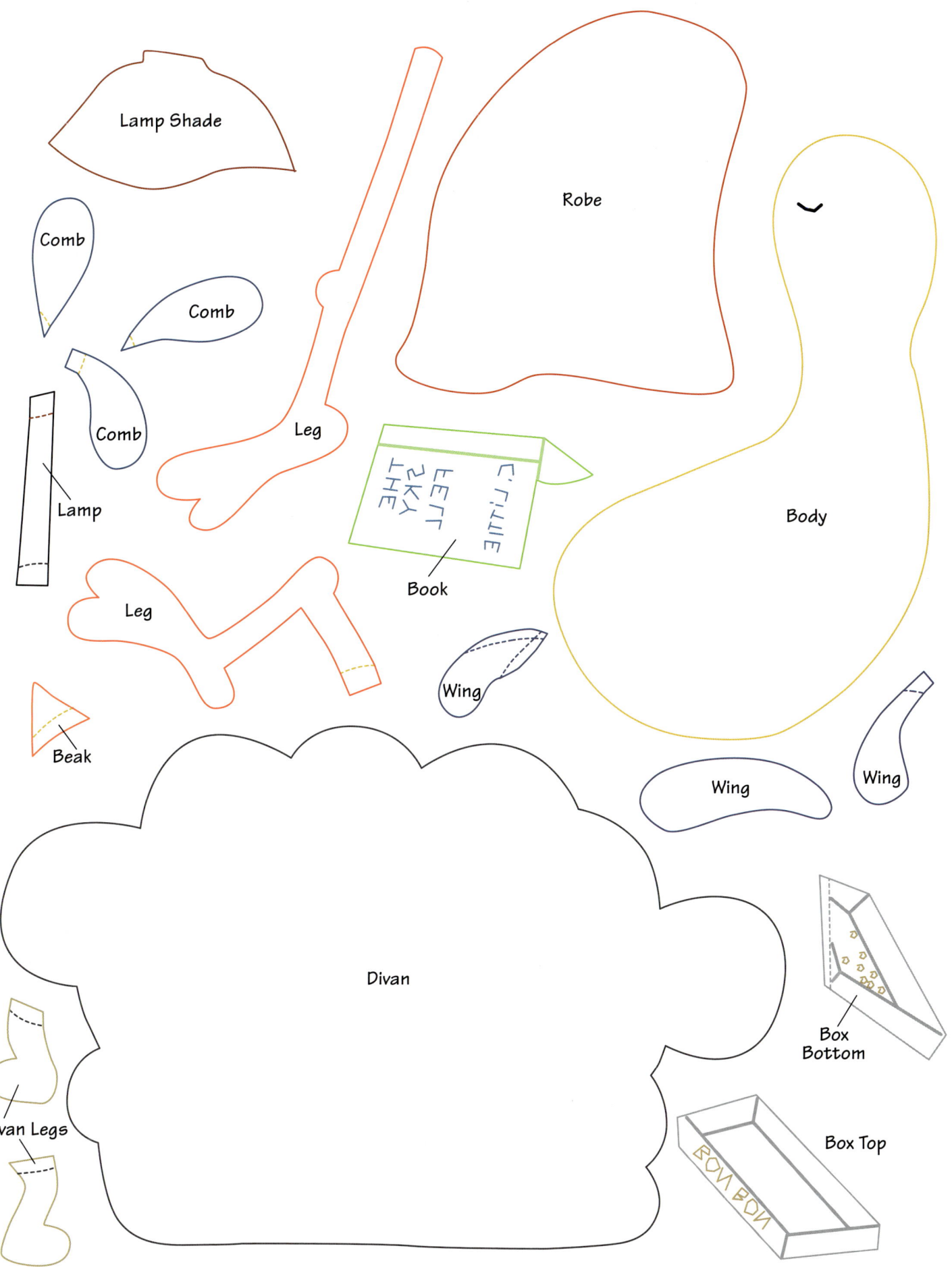

Fried Chicken

SOUTHERN FRIED CHICKEN

1 cut-up chicken
3 tsp. Lawry's Seasoned Salt
2 garlic cloves, finely chopped
1 c. all-purpose flour
1 c. vegetable oil

Sprinkle chicken with seasoned salt and garlic. Roll chicken in flour until coated, shaking off excess.

Sprinkle with additional seasoning salt to taste. In a frying pan, heat oil until very hot. Fry chicken until tender and golden brown, turning once.

Makes 4-5 servings.

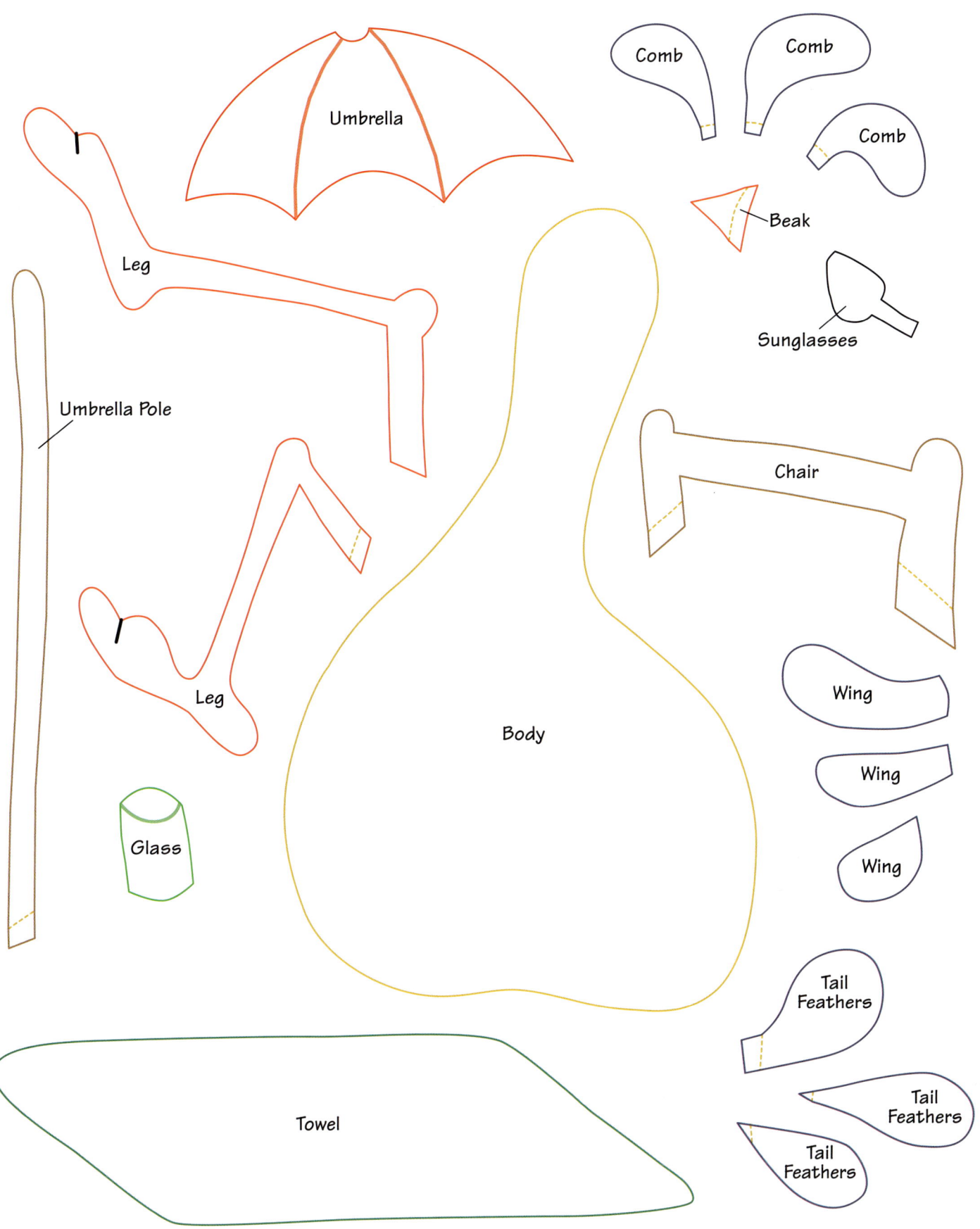

Chicken Caesar

chicken caesar

1/2 c. olive oil
2 tsp. lemon juice
1 tsp. dried tarragon leaves
1 tsp. anchovy paste
1 tsp. Worcestershire sauce
1/2 tsp. black pepper
1/4 tsp. sugar
1/4 tsp. dry mustard
1/4 tsp. salt
1/3 c. Parmesan cheese
2 garlic cloves, finely chopped
1 red sweet pepper
2 pkgs. lettuce pieces
4 whole chicken breasts, roasted and cut into bite-size pieces
1/4 lb. fresh mushrooms, thinly sliced

Note: Prepare dressing the day before or several hours before serving.

Mix first 11 ingredients in a bowl. Whisk until well blended. Set aside. Seed red pepper and cut into thin julienne strips about 1 1/2" long. Place lettuce in a large salad bowl. Add chicken, red pepper, and mushrooms. Whisk dressing and drizzle over mixture. Toss until evenly coated.

Makes 6 servings.

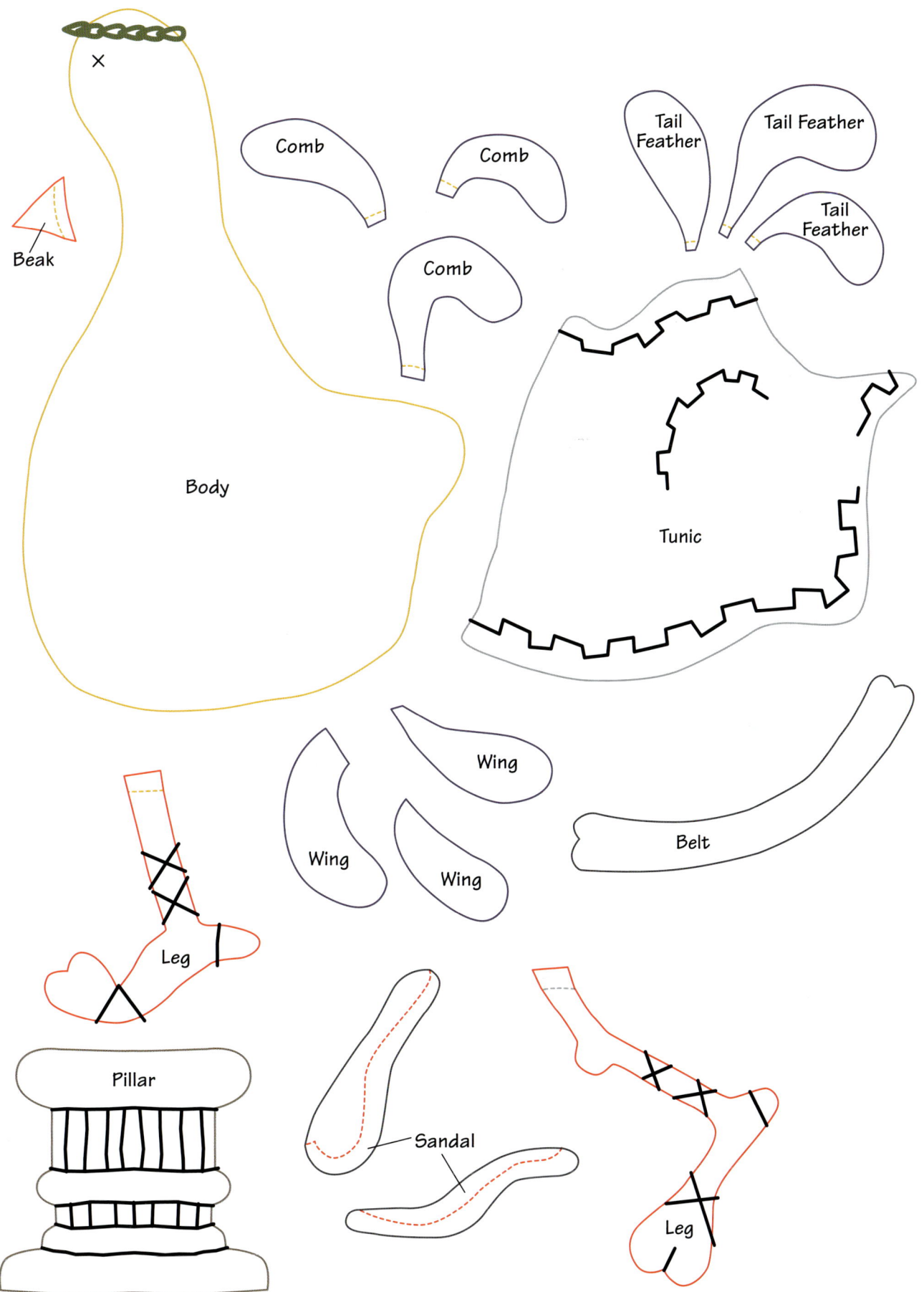

Chicken a la King

chicken a la king

3 Tbsp. butter
1 green pepper, sliced
1 c. fresh mushrooms, sliced
1 to 2 pimentos, sliced
1½ Tbsp. all-purpose flour
2 c. heavy cream, divided
½ c. chicken broth
½ c. sherry (optional)
1 tsp. salt
¼ tsp. paprika
Dash of cayenne pepper
4 egg yolks
3 c. cubed cooked chicken

Melt butter in saucepan. Add green pepper, mushrooms, and pimentos. Sauté 5 minutes. Add flour and blend well. Add ¾ c. of heavy cream and chicken broth; mix. Stirring constantly, cook over low heat until thick. Add sherry, salt, paprika, and cayenne pepper; stir.

Beat egg yolks and remaining 1¼ c. heavy cream. Slowly add cream mixture to sauce, stirring constantly. Add chicken and heat through. Do not boil.

Serve on toast or pastry shells. Makes 6 servings.

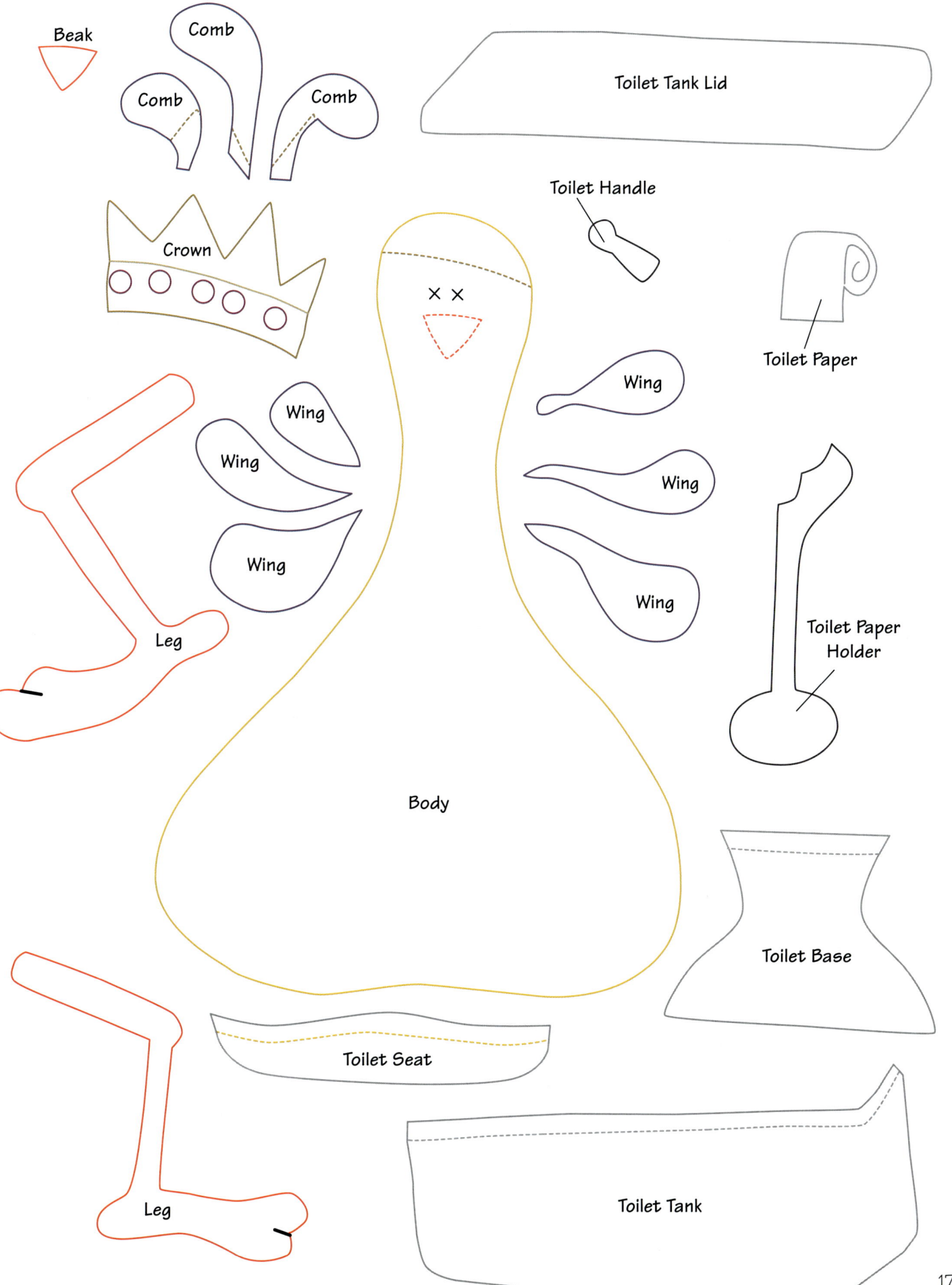

Chicken in a Basket

chicken in a basket

8-oz. pkg. cream cheese, softened
4 Tbsp. butter, softened
3 c. cubed cooked chicken
8-oz. can refrigerated crescent rolls
14-oz. can chicken broth
10¾-oz. can cream of chicken soup

Mix cream cheese and butter together; stir in chicken. Separate crescent roll dough and spoon chicken mixture on each section. Roll up each section and place on a cookie sheet. Bake in a 350° oven for 20 minutes or until lightly browned. Mix chicken broth with chicken soup; heat. Spoon over hot crescents. Can be served with rice or potatoes.

Makes 4-6 servings.

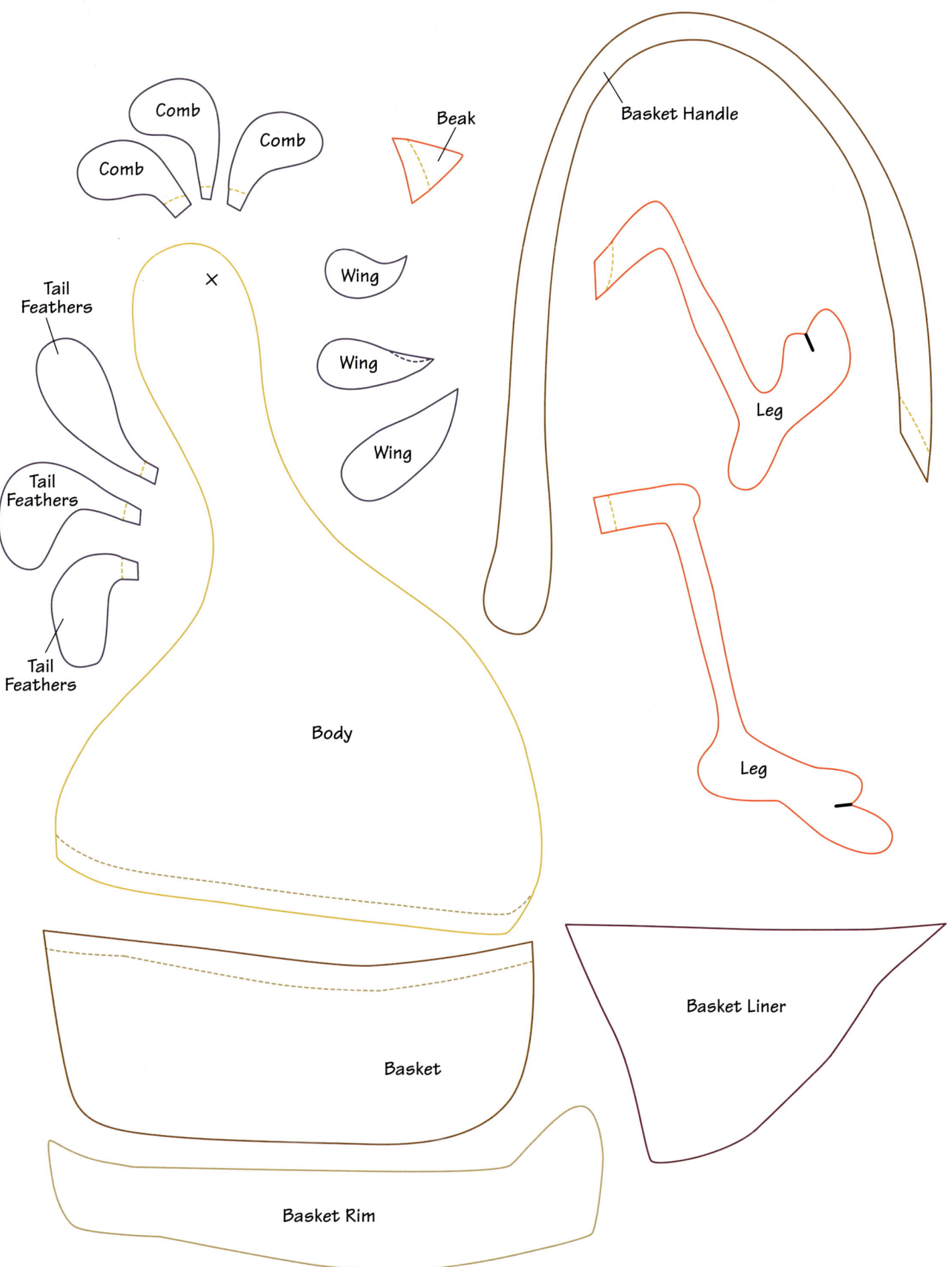

HAWAIIAN CHICKEN

4 green onions
3 - 5 Tbsp. butter, divided
4 chicken breast halves (can be skinless)
1 c. all-purpose flour, seasoned with salt and pepper
14-oz. can sliced pineapple
1 avocado, seeded and peeled
2 to 3 cups cooked white rice

Chop green part of onions. Sauté onions in 1 tablespoon of butter until glazed. Reserving butter, transfer onions to a slow cooker.

Coat chicken breast in seasoned flour. Sauté in reserved butter until brown on both sides, adding additional butter if needed to brown. Transfer to slow cooker. Saving juice, drain pineapple. Pour juice over chicken. Cover and cook on low 3-4 hours or on high for 1½-2 hours or until tender.

Sauté pineapple slices in 2 tablespoons of butter until golden. Arrange chicken breasts on plate with a pineapple slice on each. Slice avocado into 8 lengthwise strips. Place 2 strips on each pineapple slice.

Serve with rice. Pan drippings may be drizzled over rice.

Makes 4 servings.

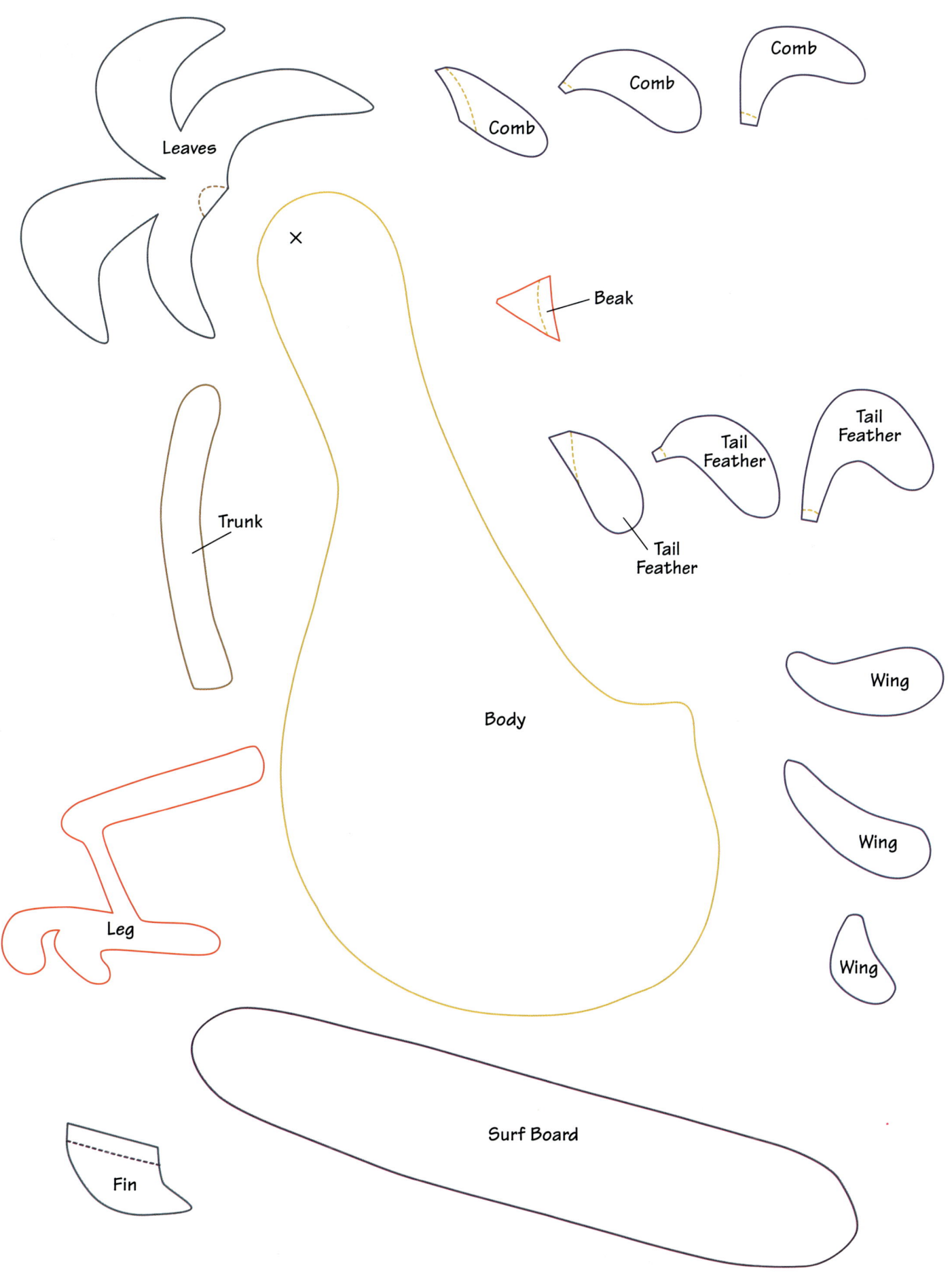

chicken chow mein

1 cut-up chicken or breast and thigh pieces
2 c. water
1 or 2 onions, chopped
1 c. celery, chopped
¼ c. cornstarch
¼ c. soy sauce
16-oz. can bean sprouts, drained
6-oz. can bamboo shoots, drained
6-oz. can water chestnuts, drained
3 Tbsp. molasses
Cooked rice or chow mein noodles

Place chicken, water, onion, and celery in a slow cooker. Cover and cook on low for about 7 hours. Turn cooker up to high and cook 1 hour more.

Leaving broth in cooker, remove chicken and debone. Cut into large pieces.

Combine cornstarch and soy sauce; whisk into broth. Add the bean sprouts, bamboo shoots, water chestnuts, and molasses; stir well. Add the chicken pieces and cook for another hour or so on high. Serve over rice or chow mein noodles.

Makes 4-6 servings.

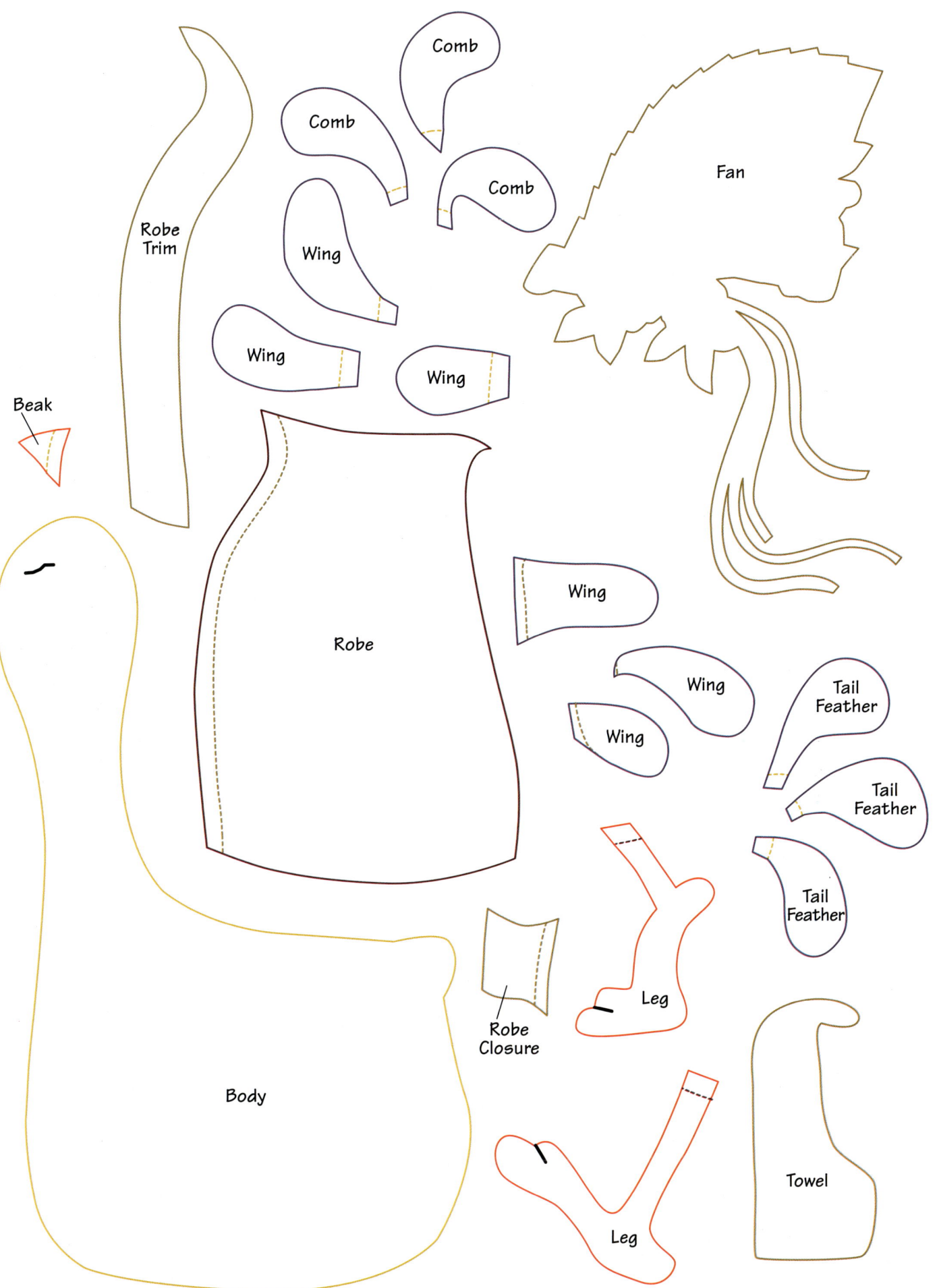

stewed chicken (with dumplings)

Chicken:
1 stewing hen
3 tsp. salt
Black pepper to taste

Dumplings:
2 c. all-purpose flour
½ tsp. salt
2 Tbsp. shortening or bacon grease
1 lg. egg
¾ c. milk

Chicken: Place chicken in deep soup/stock pot. Cover with water. Add salt and pepper. Bring to a boil. Reduce heat and cover tightly. Simmer for 2 hours or until tender. Saving broth, remove chicken and let cool. Debone chicken and cut into pieces. Refrigerate broth and skim fat (optional). Return chicken to broth. While preparing dumplings, bring broth to a boil.

Dumplings: Mix flour and salt in a bowl. Add shortening, mixing well. Beat egg into milk. Gradually add egg mixture to flour mixture until it forms a dough. Divide dough into 3 parts. Roll out each part until thin and cut into strips about 2½" x 3". Stirring constantly, drop strips, one at a time, into the boiling broth. Boil for 10 minutes.

Makes 4-6 servings.

CHICKEN SOUP

1 cut-up chicken
10 c. cold water
2 stalks celery with leaves, cut in pieces
1 onion, quartered
5 black peppercorns
6 sprigs parsley
Salt
Black pepper
1 c. vermicelli, uncooked
2 lg. eggs
Juice of 1 lemon
Carrot slivers and parsley sprigs to garnish

Place chicken in large soup/stock pot. Cover with cold water. Add celery, onion, peppercorns, and parsley to pot. Bring to a boil. Reduce heat and skim the foam from the top. Cover with lid, leaving lid slightly ajar. Simmer for 90 minutes. Let cool slightly.

Remove chicken and strain broth; return broth to pot. Add salt and pepper to broth. Debone chicken and cut into pieces. Add desired amount of the chicken back to broth. Stir in vermicelli and simmer for 15 minutes.

Beat eggs with lemon juice. Add a little of broth and stir. Stirring constantly, slowly add egg mixture back into pot. Mix well; heat through.

Garnish with carrot slivers and parsley. Makes 8 cups.

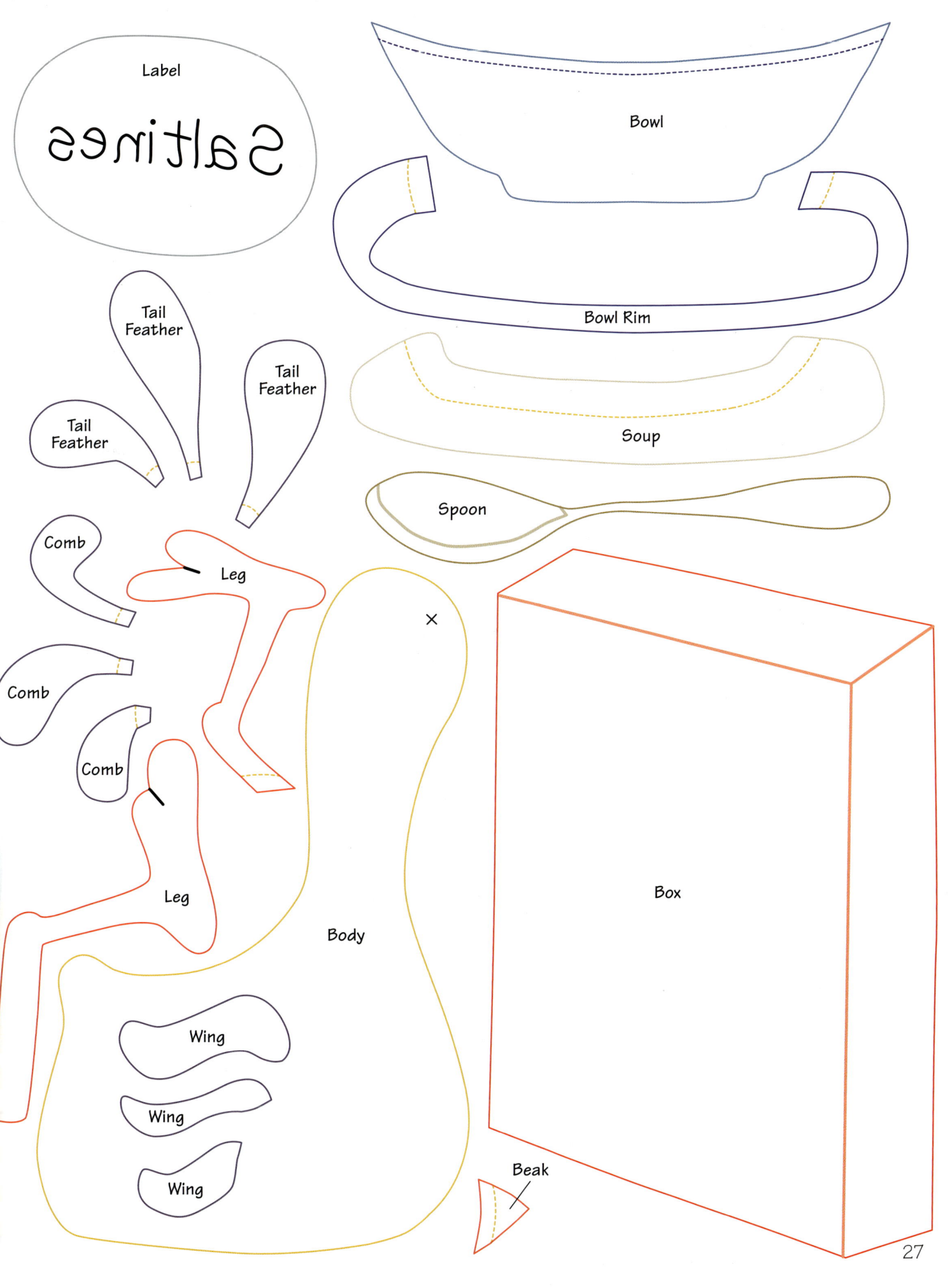

chicken italiano

14-oz. can tomatoes
½ tsp. dried basil leaves
½ tsp. dried tarragon leaves
½ tsp. salt
¼ tsp. black pepper
2 tsp. butter or vegetable oil
1 garlic clove, finely chopped
2 lbs. boneless, skinless chicken breasts
2 Tbsp. fresh parsley, chopped
 (or 2 tsp. dried parsley)
½ c. shredded mozzarella cheese

Pour tomatoes into a blender or food processor. Add basil, tarragon, salt, and pepper. Process all ingredients until smooth.

Melt butter in a large frying pen. Sauté garlic over medium heat 1 minute. Add chicken pieces; sauté, turning once until golden on both sides. Pour tomato mixture over chicken. Bring to a boil. Reduce heat and simmer 15 min. until tender.

Remove chicken and place in ovenproof serving dish. Stir parsley into sauce and spoon over chicken. Sprinkle with mozzarella cheese. Place under heated broiler to melt cheese.

Makes 4 servings.

Chicken Cacciatore

chicken cacciatore

4 boneless, skinless chicken breast halves
Non-stick cooking spray
14½-oz. can stewed tomatoes
1 c. spaghetti sauce
2½-oz. jar sliced mushrooms, drained
6-oz. uncooked linguine or fettuccini
1 Tbsp. cornstarch
1 Tbsp. cold water
2 c. frozen peppers and onions (yellow, green, and red peppers and onions)
½ c. shredded mozzarella cheese

Rinse chicken and pat dry. Spray an unheated large skillet with nonstick cooking spray. Heat over medium heat. Add chicken to skillet and cook for 5 minutes, turning once.

Add undrained stewed tomatoes, spaghetti sauce, and mushrooms. Bring to a boil. Reduce heat, cover and simmer about 15 minutes or until chicken is tender and no longer pink.

Boil linguine until tender; drain. Keep warm.

Combine cornstarch and cold water in a small bowl; add to skillet. Stirring constantly, cook until thick and bubbly. Stir in vegetables. Cook and stir for 2 minutes more. Serve over linguine. Sprinkle with mozzarella cheese.

Makes 4 servings.

30

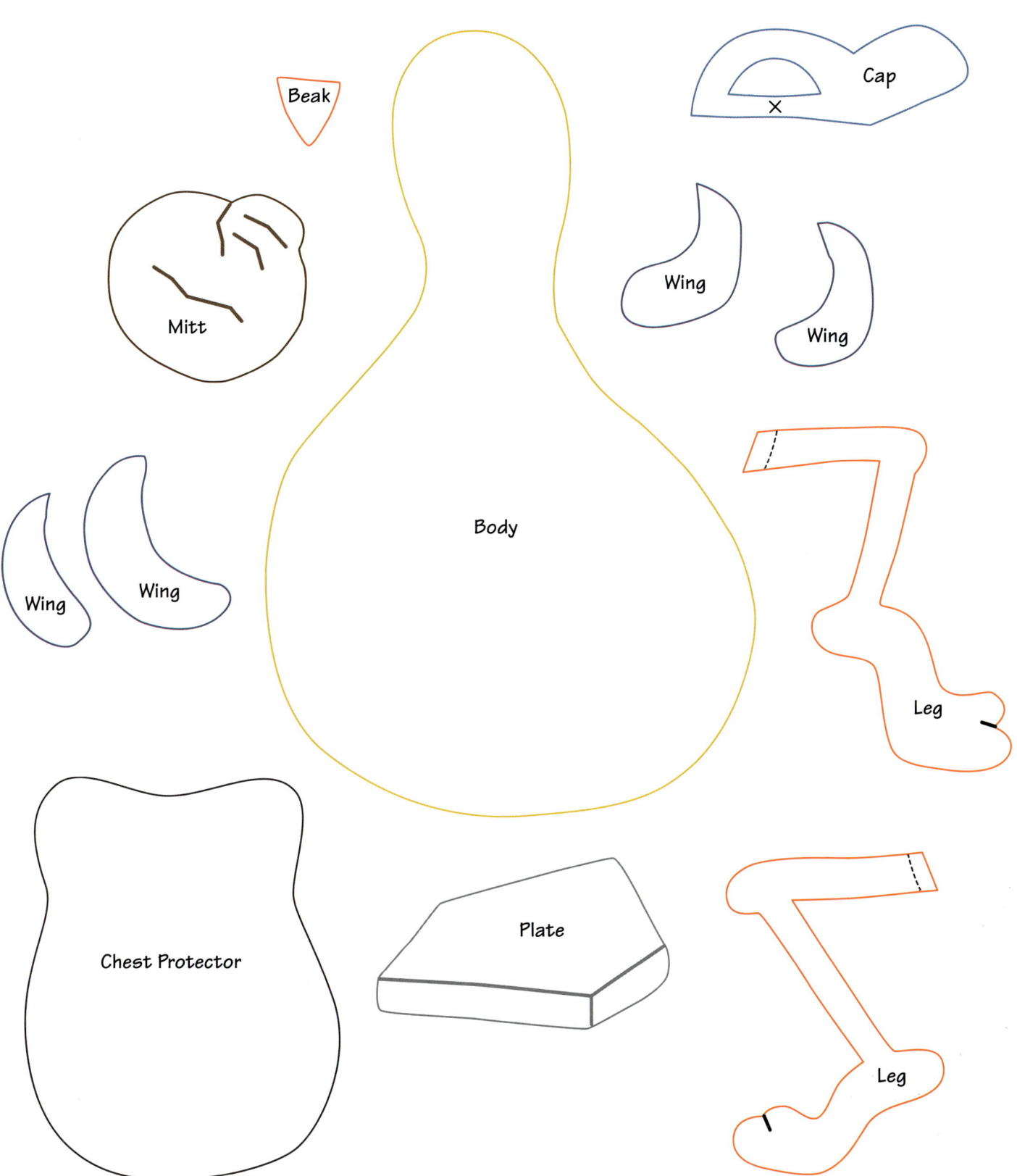

general instructions

To make your quilting easier and more enjoyable, we encourage you to carefully read all of the general instructions, study the color photographs, and familiarize yourself with the individual project instructions before beginning a project.

FABRICS

SELECTING FABRICS

Choose high-quality, medium-weight 100% cotton fabrics. All-cotton fabrics hold a crease better, fray less, and are easier to quilt than cotton/polyester blends.

Yardage requirements listed for each project are based on 43"/44" wide fabric with a "usable" width of 40" after shrinkage and trimming selvages. Actual usable width will probably vary slightly from fabric to fabric. Our recommended yardage lengths should be adequate for occasional re-squaring of fabric when many cuts are required.

PREPARING FABRICS

We recommend that all fabrics be washed, dried, and pressed before cutting. If fabrics are not pre-washed, washing the finished quilt will cause shrinkage and give it a more "antiqued" look and feel. Bright and dark colors, which may run, should always be washed before cutting. After washing and drying fabric, fold lengthwise with wrong sides together and matching selvages.

ROTARY CUTTING

Rotary cutting has brought speed and accuracy to quiltmaking by allowing quilters to easily cut strips of fabric and then cut those strips into smaller pieces.

- Place fabric on work surface with fold closest to you.

- Cut all strips from the selvage-to-selvage width of the fabric unless otherwise indicated in project instructions.

- Square left edge of fabric using rotary cutter and rulers (**Figs. 1 – 2**).

Fig. 1

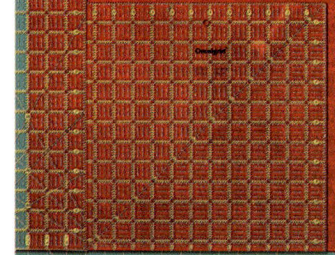

Fig. 2

- To cut each strip required for a project, place ruler over cut edge of fabric, aligning desired marking on ruler with cut edge; make cut (**Fig. 3**).

Fig. 3

- When cutting several strips from a single piece of fabric, it is important to make sure that cuts remain at a perfect right angle to the fold; square fabric as needed.

33

PIECING

Precise cutting, followed by accurate piecing, will ensure that all pieces of quilt top fit together well.

- Set sewing machine stitch length for approximately 11 stitches per inch.

- Use neutral-colored general-purpose sewing thread (not quilting thread) in needle and in bobbin.

- An accurate ¼" seam allowance is essential. Presser feet that are ¼" wide are available for most sewing machines.

- When piecing, always place pieces right sides together and match raw edges; pin if necessary.

- Chain piecing saves time and will usually result in more accurate piecing.

- Trim away points of seam allowances that extend beyond edges of sewn pieces.

SEWING ACROSS SEAM INTERSECTIONS

When sewing across intersection of two seams, place pieces right sides together and match seams exactly, making sure seam allowances are pressed in opposite directions (**Fig. 4**).

Fig. 4

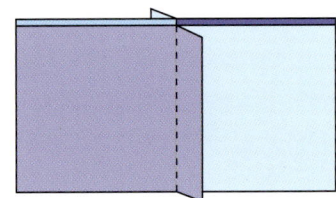

PRESSING

- Use steam iron set on "Cotton" for all pressing.

- Press after sewing each seam.

- Seam allowances are almost always pressed to one side, usually toward darker fabric. However, to reduce bulk it may occasionally be necessary to press seam allowances toward the lighter fabric or even to press them open.

- To prevent dark fabric seam allowance from showing through light fabric, trim darker seam allowance slightly narrower than lighter seam allowance.

- To press long seams, such as those in long strip sets, without curving or other distortion, lay strips across width of the ironing board.

APPLIQUÉ

PREPARING FUSIBLE APPLIQUÉS

White or light-colored fabrics may need to be lined with fusible interfacing before applying fusible web to prevent darker fabrics from showing through.

Note: On patterns, the thin solid outer lines (——) are tracing/cutting lines. The dashed lines (- - -) are overlap lines. The wide solid lines (——) are for embroidery placement.

1. Place paper-backed fusible web, paper side up, over appliqué pattern. Trace pattern onto paper side of web with pencil as many times as indicated in project instructions for a single fabric.
2. Follow manufacturer's instructions to fuse traced patterns to wrong side of fabrics. Do not remove paper backing.
3. Use scissors to cut out appliqué pieces along traced lines. Remove paper backing from all pieces.

MACHINE BLANKET STITCH APPLIQUÉ

Some sewing machines feature a Blanket Stitch similar to the one used in this book. Refer to your owner's manual for machine set-up. If your machine does not have this stitch, try any of the decorative stitches your machine has until you are satisfied with the look.

1. Thread sewing machine and bobbin with 100% cotton thread in desired weight.
2. Attach an open-toe presser foot. Select far right needle position and needle down (if your machine has these features).
3. If desired, pin a commercial stabilizer to wrong side of background fabric or spray wrong side of background fabric with starch to stabilize.
4. Bring bobbin thread to the top of the fabric by lowering then raising the needle, bringing up the bobbin thread loop. Pull the loop all the way to the surface.
5. Begin by stitching 5 or 6 stitches in place (drop feed dogs or set stitch length at 0), or use your machine's lock stitch feature, if equipped, to anchor thread. Return setting to selected Blanket Stitch.

6. Most of the Blanket Stitch should be done on the appliqué with the right edges of the stitch falling at the very outside edge of the appliqué. Stitch over all exposed raw edges of appliqué pieces.
7. (*Note:* Dots on **Figs. 5 - 9** indicate where to leave needle in fabric when pivoting.) Always stopping with needle down in background fabric, refer to **Fig. 5** to stitch outside points like tips of leaves. Stop one stitch short of point. Raise presser foot. Pivot project slightly, lower presser foot, and make one angled Stitch 1. Take next stitch, stop at point, and pivot so Stitch 2 will be perpendicular to point. Pivot slightly to make Stitch 3. Continue stitching.

Fig. 5

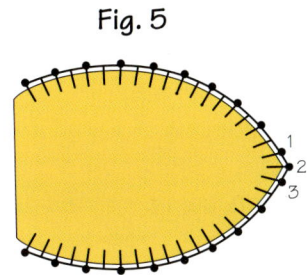

8. For outside corners (**Fig. 6**), stitch to corner, stopping with needle in background fabric. Raise presser foot. Pivot project, lower presser foot, and take an angled stitch. Raise presser foot. Pivot project, lower presser foot and stitch adjacent side.

Fig. 6

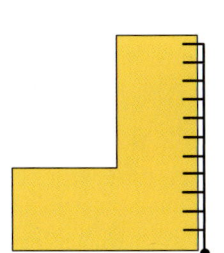 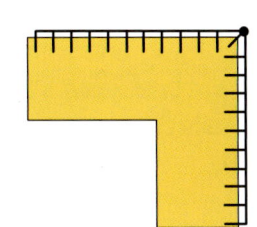

9. For inside corners (**Fig. 7**), stitch to the corner, taking the last bite at corner and stopping with the needle down in background fabric. Raise presser foot. Pivot project, lower presser foot, and take an angled stitch. Raise presser foot. Pivot project, lower presser foot and stitch adjacent side.

Fig. 7

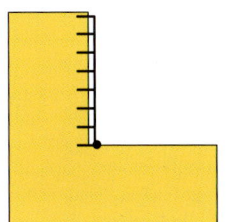 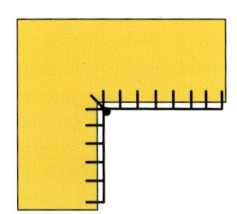

10. When stitching outside curves (**Fig. 8**), stop with needle down in background fabric. Raise presser foot and pivot project as needed. Lower presser foot and continue stitching, pivoting as often as necessary to follow curve. Small circles may require pivoting between each stitch.

Fig. 8

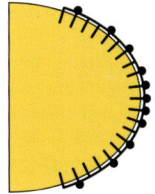

11. When stitching inside curves (**Fig. 9**), stop with needle down in background fabric. Raise presser foot and pivot project as needed. Lower presser foot and continue stitching, pivoting as often as necessary to follow curve.

Fig. 9

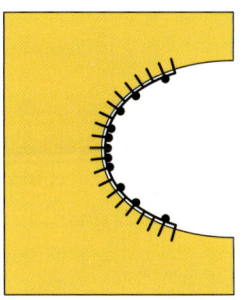

12. When stopping stitching, use a lock stitch to sew 5 or 6 stitches in place or use a needle to pull threads to wrong side of background fabric (**Fig. 10**); knot, then trim ends.

Fig. 10

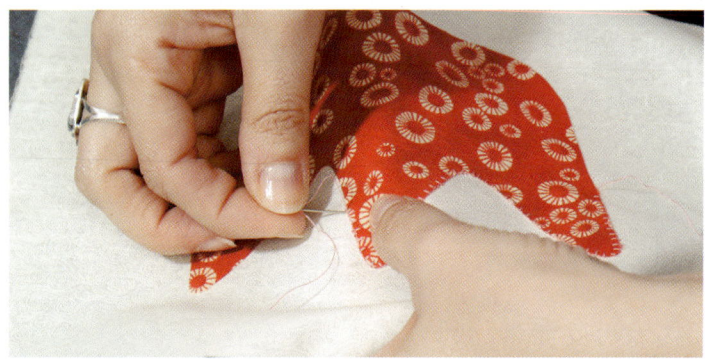

13. Carefully tear away stabilizer, if used.

QUILTING

Quilting holds the three layers (top, batting, and backing) of the quilt together and can be done by hand or machine. Because marking, layering, and quilting are interrelated and may be done in different orders depending on circumstances, please read entire Quilting section, pages 36 – 38, before beginning project.

TYPES OF QUILTING DESIGNS

In the Ditch Quilting
Quilting along seamlines or along edges of appliquéd pieces is called "in the ditch" quilting. This type of quilting should be done on side opposite seam allowance and does not have to be marked.

Outline Quilting
Quilting a consistent distance, usually $1/4$", from seam or appliqué is called "outline" quilting. Outline quilting may be marked, or $1/4$" masking tape may be placed along seamlines for quilting guide. (Do not leave tape on quilt longer than necessary, since it may leave an adhesive residue.)

Motif Quilting
Quilting a design, such as a feathered wreath, is called "motif" quilting. This type of quilting should be marked before basting quilt layers together.

Echo Quilting
Quilting that follows the outline of an appliquéd or pieced design with two or more parallel lines is called "echo" quilting. This type of quilting does not need to be marked.

Meandering Quilting
Quilting in random curved lines and swirls is called "meandering" quilting. Quilting lines should not cross or touch each other. This type of quilting does not need to be marked.

MARKING QUILTING LINES
Quilting lines may be marked using fabric marking pencils, chalk markers, water- or air-soluble pens, or lead pencils.

Simple quilting designs may be marked with chalk or chalk pencil after basting. A small area may be marked, then quilted, before moving to next area to be marked. Intricate designs should be marked before basting using a more durable marker.

Caution: Pressing may permanently set some marks. Test different markers on scrap fabric to find one that marks clearly and can be thoroughly removed.

A wide variety of pre-cut quilting stencils, as well as entire books of quilting patterns, are available. Using a stencil makes it easier to mark intricate or repetitive designs.

To make a stencil from a pattern, center template plastic over pattern and use a permanent marker to trace pattern onto plastic. Use a craft knife with single or double blade to cut channels along traced lines (**Fig. 11**).

Fig. 11

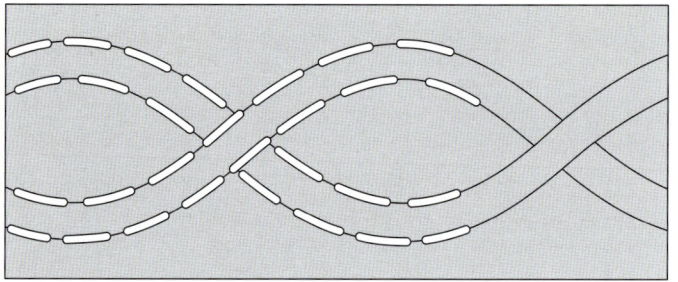

CHOOSING THE BATTING

The appropriate batting will make quilting easier. For fine hand quilting, choose low-loft batting. All cotton or cotton/polyester blend battings work well for machine quilting because the cotton helps "grip" quilt layers. If quilt is to be tied, a high-loft batting, sometimes called extra-loft or fat batting, may be used to make quilt "fluffy."

Types of batting include cotton, polyester, wool, silk cotton/polyester blend and cotton/wool blend.

When selecting batting, refer to package labels for characteristics and care instructions. Cut batting same size as prepared backing.

PREPARING THE BACKING

To allow for slight shifting of quilt top during quilting, backing should be approximately 4" larger on all sides. Yardage requirements listed for quilt backings are calculated for 43"/44"w fabric. Using 90"w fabric for the backing may eliminate piecing. To piece a backing using 43"/44"w fabric, use the following instructions.

1. Measure length and width of quilt top; add 8" to each measurement.
2. Cut backing fabric into 2 or 3 lengths (depending on quilt size) the determined length measurement. Trim selvages. Place lengths with right sides facing and sew long edges together, forming tube (**Fig. 12**). Match seams and press along one fold (**Fig. 13**). Cut along pressed fold to form single piece (**Fig. 14**).

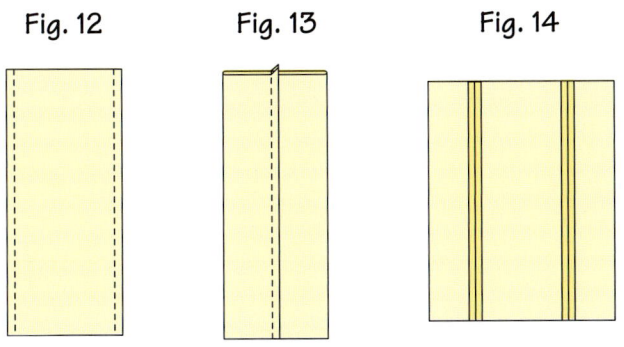

Fig. 12　　Fig. 13　　Fig. 14

3. Trim backing to size determined in Step 1; press seam allowances open.

ASSEMBLING THE QUILT

1. Examine wrong side of quilt top closely; trim any seam allowances and clip any threads that may show through front of the quilt. Press quilt top, being careful not to "set" any marked quilting lines.
2. Place backing wrong side up on flat surface. Use masking tape to tape edges of backing to surface. Place batting on top of backing fabric. Smooth batting gently, being careful not to stretch or tear. Center quilt top right side up on batting.
3. Use 1" rustproof safety pins to "pin-baste" all layers together, spacing pins approximately 4" apart. Begin at center and work toward outer edges to secure all layers. If possible, place pins away from areas that will be quilted, although pins may be removed as needed when quilting.

MACHINE QUILTING METHODS

Use general-purpose thread in bobbin. Do not use quilting thread. Thread the needle of machine with general-purpose thread or transparent monofilament thread to make quilting blend with quilt top fabrics. Use decorative thread, such as a metallic or contrasting-color general-purpose thread, to make quilting lines stand out more.

Straight-Line Quilting

The term "straight-line" is somewhat deceptive, since curves (especially gentle ones) as well as straight lines can be stitched with this technique.

1. Set stitch length for six to ten stitches per inch and attach walking foot to sewing machine.
2. Determine which section of quilt will have longest continuous quilting line, oftentimes area from center top to center bottom. Roll up and secure each edge of quilt to help reduce the bulk, keeping fabrics smooth. Smaller projects may not need to be rolled.
3. Begin stitching on longest quilting line, using very short stitches for the first $1/4$" to "lock" quilting. Stitch across project, using one hand on each side of walking foot to slightly spread fabric and to guide fabric through machine. Lock stitches at end of quilting line.
4. Continue machine quilting, stitching longer quilting lines first to stabilize quilt before moving on to other areas.

Free-Motion Quilting

Free-motion quilting may be free form or may follow a marked pattern.
1. Attach darning foot to sewing machine and lower or cover feed dogs.
2. Position quilt under darning foot; lower foot. Holding top thread, take a stitch and pull bobbin thread to top of quilt. To "lock" beginning of quilting line, hold top and bobbin threads while making three to five stitches in place.
3. Use one hand on each side of darning foot to slightly spread fabric and to move fabric through the machine. Even stitch length is achieved by using smooth, flowing hand motion and steady machine speed. Slow machine speed and fast hand movement will create long stitches. Fast machine speed and slow hand movement will create short stitches. Move quilt sideways, back and forth, in a circular motion, or in a random motion to create desired designs; do not rotate quilt. Lock stitches at end of each quilting line.

MAKING A HANGING SLEEVE

Attaching a hanging sleeve to back of wall hanging or quilt before the binding is added allows project to be displayed on wall.
1. Measure width of quilt top edge and subtract 1". Cut piece of fabric 7"w by determined measurement.
2. Press short edges of fabric piece 1/4" to wrong side; press edges 1/4" to wrong side again and machine stitch in place.
3. Matching wrong sides, fold piece in half lengthwise to form tube.
4. Follow project instructions to sew binding to quilt top and to trim backing and batting. Before Blindstitching binding to backing, match raw edges and stitch hanging sleeve to center top edge on back of quilt.
5. Finish binding quilt, treating hanging sleeve as part of backing.
6. Blindstitch bottom of hanging sleeve to backing, taking care not to stitch through to front of quilt.

BINDING

1. Using a diagonal seam (**Fig. 15**), sew binding strips together end to end.

Fig. 15

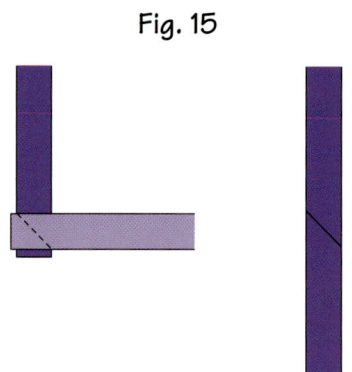

2. Matching wrong sides and raw edges, press strip(s) in half lengthwise.
3. Beginning with one end near center on bottom edge of quilt, lay binding around quilt to make sure that seams in binding will not end up at a corner. Adjust placement if necessary. Matching raw edges of binding to raw edge of quilt top, pin binding to right side of quilt along one edge.
4. When you reach first corner, mark 1/4" from corner of quilt top (**Fig. 16**).

Fig. 16

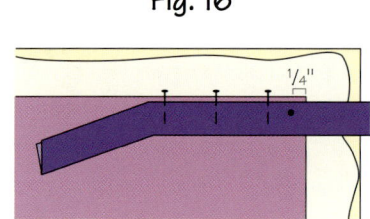

5. Beginning approximately 10" from end of binding and using ¼" seam allowance, sew binding to quilt, backstitching at beginning of stitching and at mark (**Fig. 17**). Lift needle out of fabric and clip thread.

Fig. 17

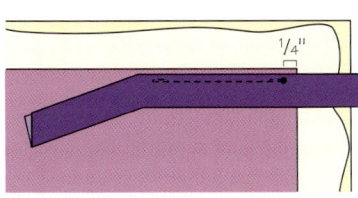

6. Fold binding as shown in **Figs. 18 – 19** and pin binding to adjacent side, matching raw edges. When you've reached the next corner, mark ¼" from edge of quilt top.

Fig. 18   Fig. 19

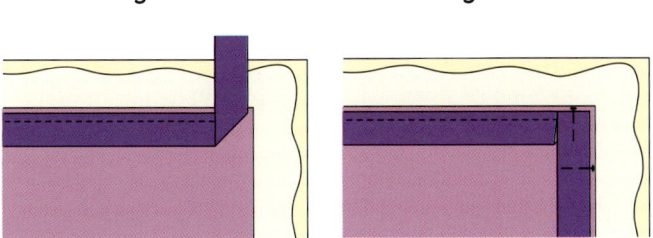

7. Backstitching at edge of quilt top, sew pinned binding to quilt (**Fig. 20**); backstitch at the next mark. Lift needle out of fabric and clip thread.

Fig. 20

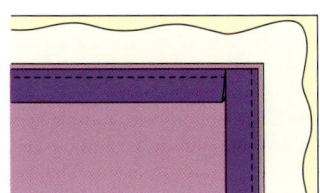

8. Continue sewing binding to quilt, stopping approximately 10" from starting point (**Fig. 21**).

Fig. 21

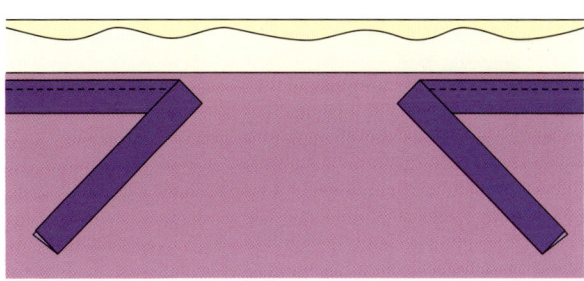

9. Bring beginning and end of binding to center of opening and fold each end back, leaving a ¼" space between folds (**Fig. 22**). Finger press folds.

Fig. 22

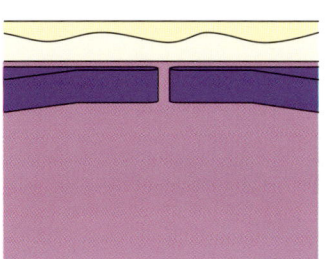

10. Unfold ends of binding and draw a line across wrong side in finger-pressed crease. Draw a line through the lengthwise pressed fold of binding at the same spot to create a cross mark. With edge of ruler at cross mark, line up 45° angle marking on ruler with one long side of binding. Draw a diagonal line from edge to edge. Repeat on remaining end, making sure that the two diagonal lines are angled the same way (**Fig. 23**).

Fig. 23

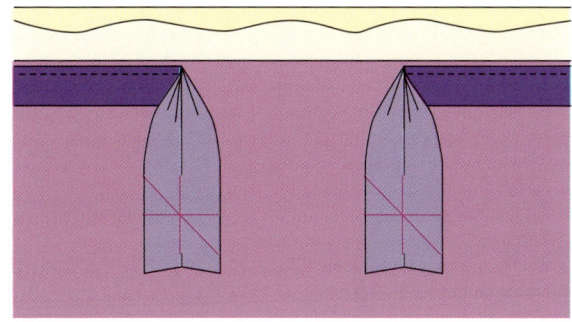

11. Matching right sides and diagonal lines, pin binding ends together a right angles (**Fig. 24**).

39

Fig. 24

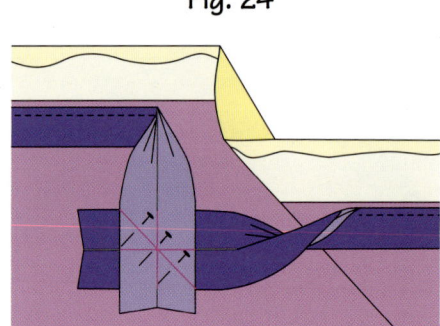

12. Machine stitch along diagonal line (**Fig. 25**), removing pins as you stitch.

Fig. 25

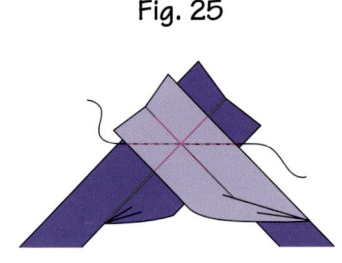

13. Lay binding against quilt to double check that it is correct length.
14. Trim binding ends, leaving 1/4" seam allowance; press seam open. Stitch binding to quilt.
15. Trim backing and batting a scant 1/4" larger than quilt top so that batting and backing will fill the binding when it is folded over to quilt backing. If using narrower binding, trim backing and batting even with edges of quilt top.
16. On one edge of quilt, fold binding over to quilt backing and pin pressed edge in place, covering stitching line (**Fig. 26**). On adjacent side, fold binding over, forming a mitered corner (**Fig. 27**). Repeat to pin remainder of binding in place.

Fig. 26   **Fig. 27**

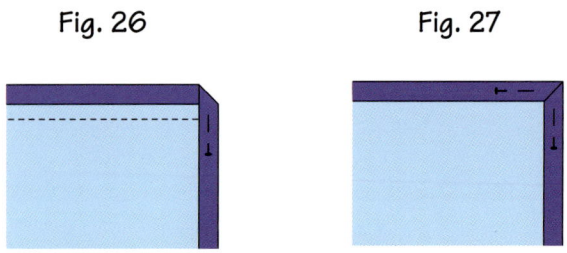

17. Blindstitch binding to backing, taking care not to stitch through to front of quilt.

SIGNING AND DATING YOUR QUILT

A completed quilt is a work of art and should be signed and dated. There are many different ways to do this and numerous books on the subject. The label should reflect the style of the quilt, the occasion or person for which it was made, and the quilter's own particular talents. Following are suggestions for recording the history of quilt or adding a sentiment for future generations.

- Embroider quilter's name, date, and any additional information on quilt top or backing. Matching floss, such as cream floss on white border, will leave a subtle record. Bright or contrasting floss will make the information stand out.

- Make label from muslin and use permanent marker to write information. Use different colored permanent markers to make label more decorative. Stitch label to back of quilt.

- Use photo-transfer paper to add image to white or cream fabric label. Stitch label to back of quilt.

- Piece an extra block from quilt top pattern to use as label. Add information with permanent fabric pen. Appliqué block to back of quilt.

- Write message on appliquéd design from quilt top. Attach appliqué to back of the quilt.

HAND STITCHES
BACK STITCH

Come up at 1, go down at 2, and come up at 3 (**Fig. 28**). Length of stitches may be varied as desired.

Fig. 28

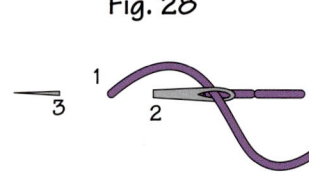

40

BLINDSTITCH

Come up at 1, go down at 2, and come up at 3 (**Fig. 29**). Length of stitches may be varied as desired.

Fig. 29

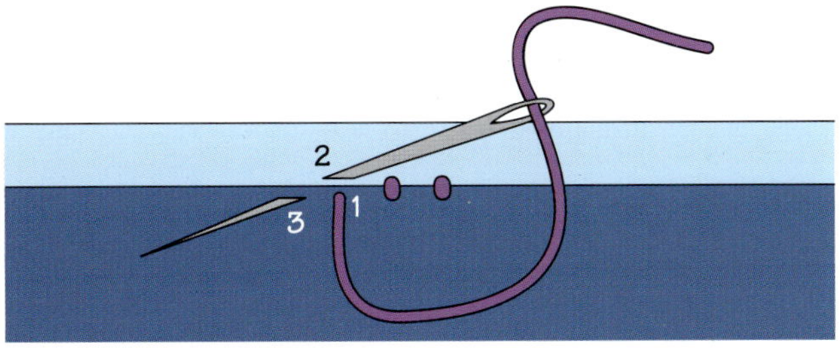

CHAIN STITCH

Come up at 1 and go down again at 1 to form a loop (**Fig. 30**). Keeping loop below point of needle, come up at 2 and go down again at 2 to form second loop. Continue making loops or "chain" until reaching end of line. Tack last loop (**Fig. 31**).

Fig. 30   Fig. 31

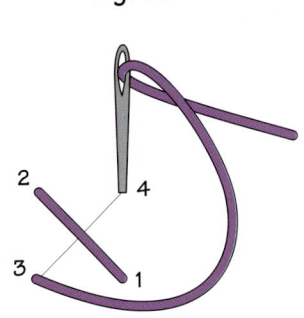

CROSS STITCH

Come up at 1 and go down at 2. Come up at 3 and go down at 4 (**Fig. 32**).

Fig. 32

FRENCH KNOT

Follow **Figs. 33 – 36** to complete French Knots. Come up at 1. Wrap thread once around needle and insert needle at 2, holding end of thread with non-stitching fingers. Tighten knot, then pull needle through, holding floss until it must be released.

Fig. 33   Fig. 34

Fig. 35   Fig. 36

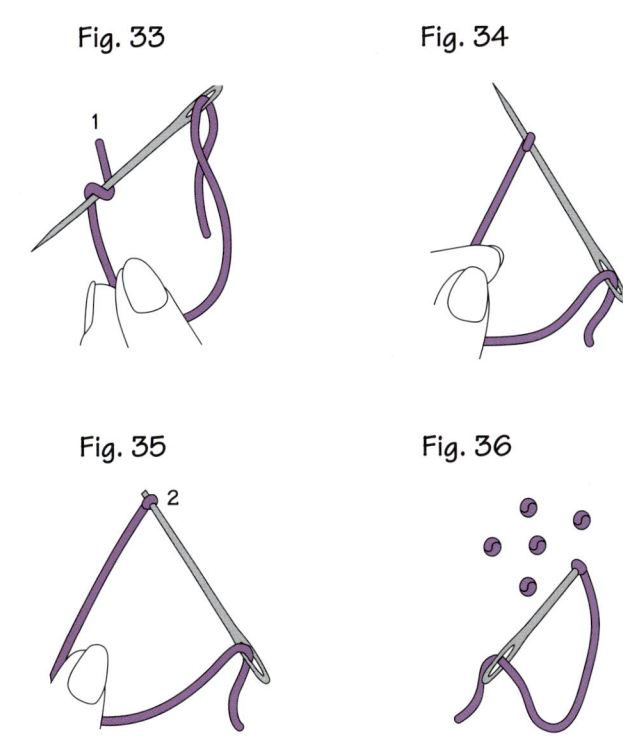

STEM STITCH

Come up at 1. Keeping thread below the stitching line, go down at 2 and come up at 3. Go down at 4 and come up at 5 (**Fig. 34**).

Fig. 34

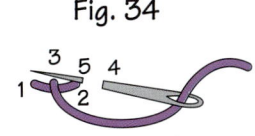

STRAIGHT STITCH

Come up at 1 and go down at 2 (**Fig. 35**). Length of stitches may be varied as desired.

Fig. 35

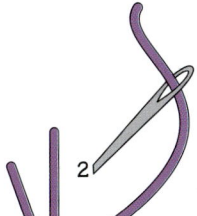

metric conversion chart

Metric Conversion Chart	
Inches x 2.54 = centimeters (cm)	Yards x .9144 = meters (m)
Inches x 25.4 = millimeters (mm)	Yards x 91.44 = centimeters (cm)
Inches x .0254 = meters (m)	Centimeters x .3937 = inches (")
	Meters x 1.0936 = yards (yd)

Standard Equivalents

1/8"	3.2 mm	0.32 cm	1/8 yard	11.43 cm	0.11 m
1/4"	6.35 mm	0.635 cm	1/4 yard	22.86 cm	0.23 m
3/8"	9.5 mm	0.95 cm	3/8 yard	34.29 cm	0.34 m
1/2"	12.7 mm	1.27 cm	1/2 yard	45.72 cm	0.46 m
5/8"	15.9 mm	1.59 cm	5/8 yard	57.15 cm	0.57 m
3/4"	19.1 mm	1.91 cm	3/4 yard	68.58 cm	0.69 m
7/8"	22.2 mm	2.22 cm	7/8 yard	80 cm	0.8 m
1"	25.4 mm	2.54 cm	1 yard	91.44 cm	0.91 m

production team:

Technical Editor – Lisa Lancaster
Technical Writer – Jean Lewis
Senior Graphic Artist – Lora Puls
Graphic Artists – Elaine Wheat,
  Janie Wright, and Amy Temple
Photography Stylist – Jessica Wurst
Photographer – Jason Masters

Copyright © 2008 by Leisure Arts, Inc., 5701 Ranch Drive, Little Rock, AR 72223. All rights reserved. This publication is protected under federal copyright laws. Reproduction or distribution of this publication or any other Leisure Arts publication, including publications which are out of print, is prohibited unless specifically authorized. This includes, but is not limited to, any form of reproduction or distribution on or through the Internet, including posting, scanning, or e-mail transmission.

We have made every effort to ensure that these instructions and recipes are accurate and complete. We cannot, however, be responsible for human error, typographical mistakes, or variations in individual work.

Discover the world of Leisure Arts Publications where inspiration lives on every page.

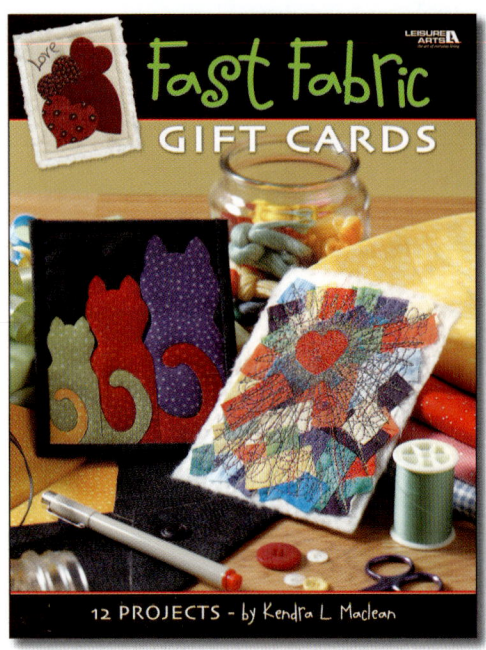

Leaflet #3997

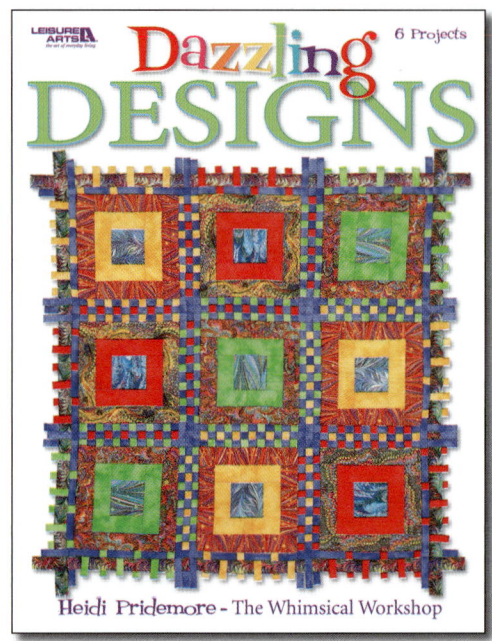

Leaflet #3940

Your next great idea starts here.

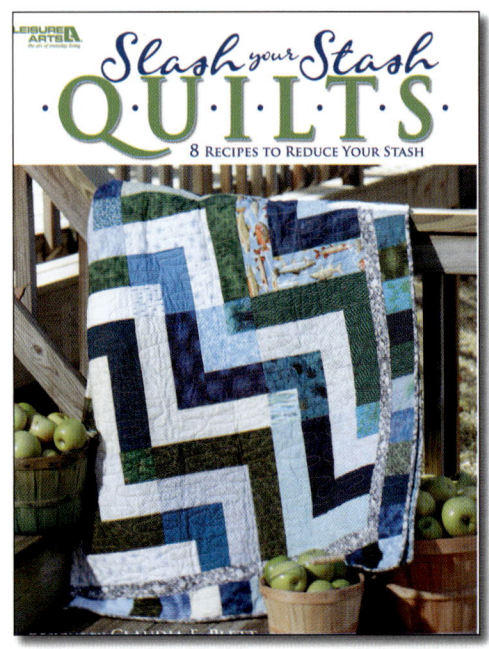

Leaflet #4219

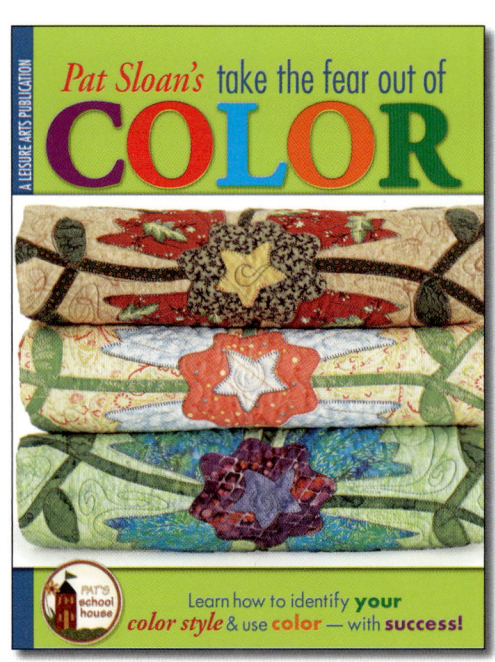

Leaflet #4286

Visit your favorite retailer, or shop online at **leisurearts.com**.
For more inspiration, sign up for our free e-newsletter and receive free projects, reviews of our newest books, handy tips and more. Have questions? Call us at 1-800-526-5111.